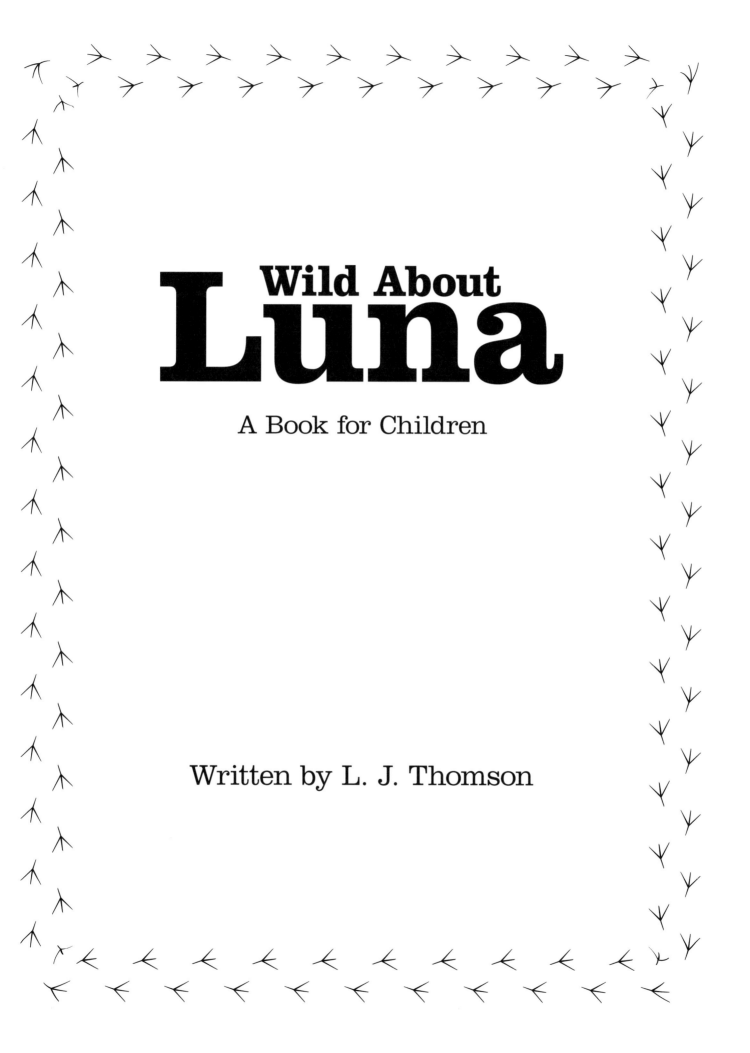

Wild About Luna

A Book for Children

Written by L. J. Thomson

Archway Publishing books may be ordered through booksellers or by contacting:

Archway Publishing
1663 Liberty Drive
Bloomington, IN 47403
www.archwaypublishing.com
1 (888) 242-5904

ISBN: 978-1-4808-7905-8 (sc)
ISBN: 978-1-4808-7904-1 (hc)
ISBN: 978-1-4808-7906-5 (e)

Print information available on the last page.

Archway Publishing rev. date: 7/12/2019

ARCHWAY
PUBLISHING

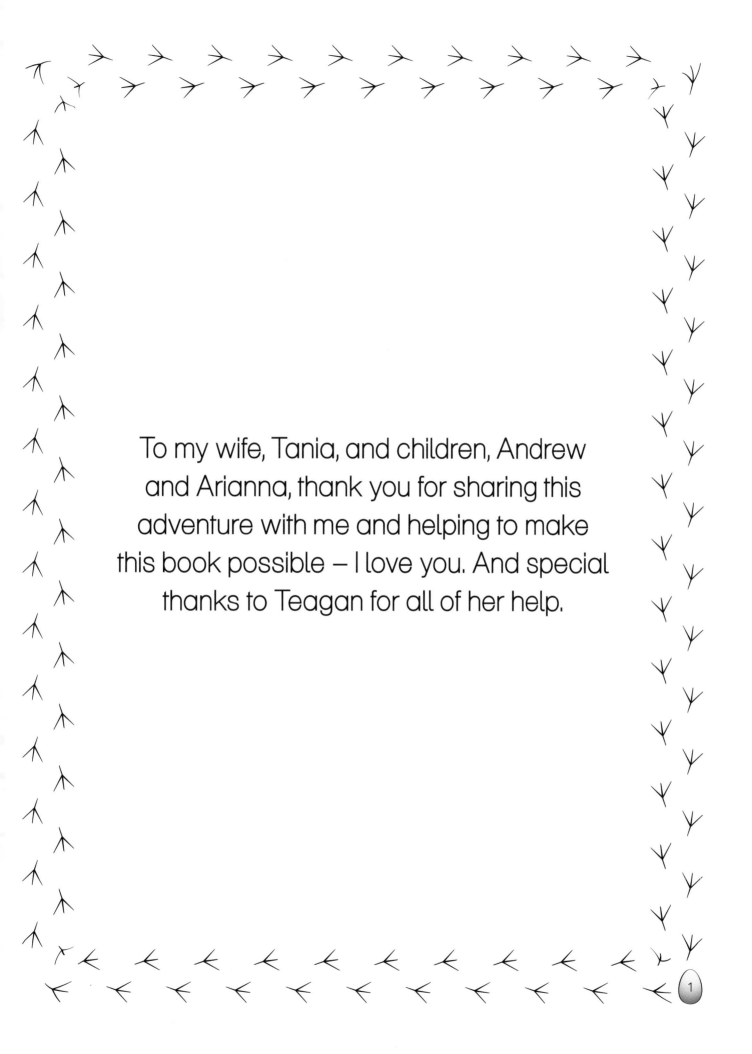

To my wife, Tania, and children, Andrew and Arianna, thank you for sharing this adventure with me and helping to make this book possible – I love you. And special thanks to Teagan for all of her help.

As far back as Luna could remember, she had always been able to run faster and fly farther than her brothers and sisters.

3

After all, Luna was a very special
bird—and not just any bird.
Luna was a wild turkey.

On Beacon Hill, the breeze was warm and steady, the days were sunny, and everything was new and waiting to be explored. Life on the hill was good.

Luna had never met anyone from beyond the hill. One day, a strange bird came to the hill. He stayed for a while but then moved on.

Before long, Luna and her sisters
were ready to fill their nests with eggs.
Luna wanted to be a mother.

To care for her eggs, Luna had to sleep on the ground in her nest at night instead of in the trees. Life in a nest on the ground could be dangerous for a wild turkey.

One night, trouble came in the form of a red fox. The fox had its own family and needed food. That night, Luna lost one of her sisters.

But Luna had a sharp beak and strong wings that she could use to protect herself and her eggs. Luna was injured by the fox that night, but she had a family of her own to protect. And she did.

The fox soon left, and Luna went back to her nest. Luna looked forward to having her own family. And she did.

Soon Luna's eggs hatched, and the
days were again warm and sunny on
the hill. Luna's babies grew quickly.

Luna was a good mother. Days were spent exploring the hill and teaching her babies all that she knew. This, of course, included finding and eating her favorite food, blueberries.

Luna's babies could now run fast and fly far. And they did. But that was no surprise. After all, they were just like Luna.

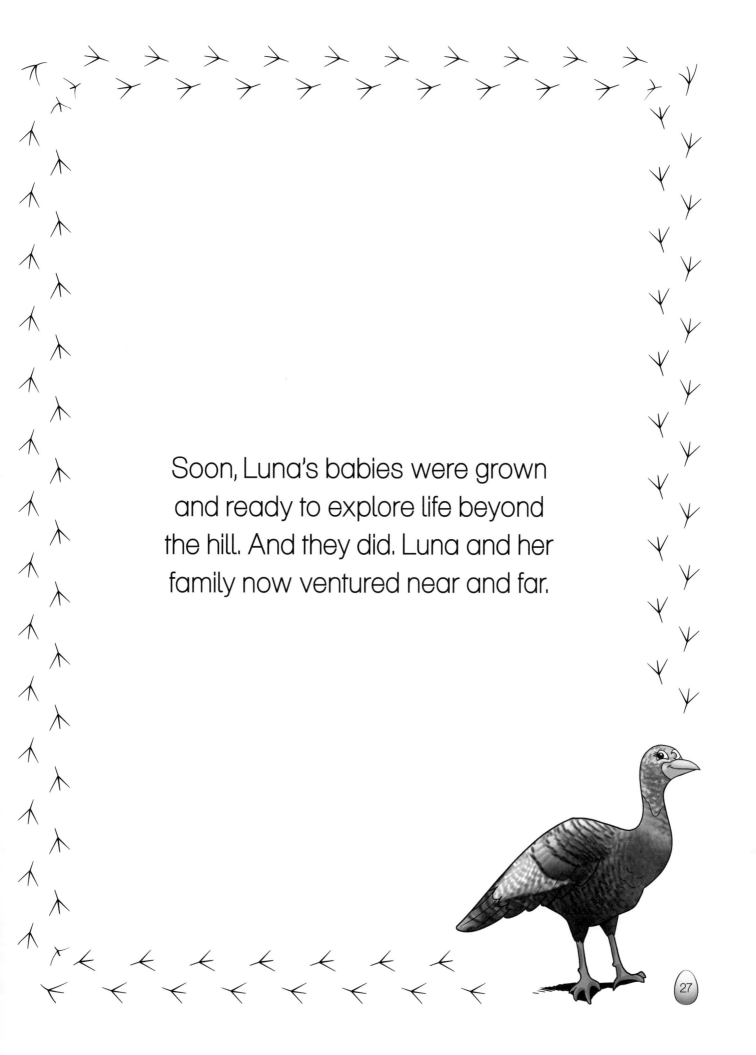

Soon, Luna's babies were grown and ready to explore life beyond the hill. And they did. Luna and her family now ventured near and far.

Luna was happy. She had seen many
things and visited many places, but
Luna decided to return to the hill.
She liked it there. After all, it was her
home and a very good place to live,
especially if you are a wild turkey.

The End

Arianna with Luna's baby

Tania with the flock

Andrew with the flock

The author with Luna

Printed in the United States
By Bookmasters